P9-DTL-181

TABLE OF CONTENTS

INTRODUCTION: A NEW GOVERNMENT WITH THREE BRANCHES

QUICK QUESTIONS: Suppose you were part of a brand new country. What would you do if that country's government just couldn't agree on what laws to make? How would the new government keep one person from taking too much power?

America was in that situation in 1787. The states were not united in most ways. Eleven years earlier, in 1776, thirteen American colonies had declared

(Above) Many future American leaders signed the Declaration of Independence.

A BALANCING ACT

A LOOK AT CHECKS AND BALANCES

By Kathiann M. Kowalski

LERNER PUBLICATIONS COMPANY • MINNEAPOLIS

This book is dedicated to my daughter, Bethany Lynn Meissner.

The author gratefully acknowledges the helpful comments offered by Michael Meissner, Laura Meissner, Chris Meissner, Bethany Meissner, Kenneth Moore, and Terrence Perris.

Lerner Publications Company
A division of Lerner Publishing Group
241 First Avenue North
Minneapolis, MN 55401 U.S.A.

Website address: www.lernerbooks.com

Library of Congress Cataloging-in-Publication Data

Kowalski, Kathiann M., 1955–
    A Balancing Act: A Look at Checks and Balances / by Kathiann M. Kowalski.
       p.   cm. — (How government works)
    Includes bibliographical references and index.
    Contents: A new government with three branches—Congress at work—The president and the veto power—The courts and judicial review—Checks on the judiciary—Impeachment—The states and the people.
      ISBN: 0–8225–1350–1 (lib. bdg. : alk. paper)
    1. Separation of powers—United States—Juvenile literature. 2. United States—Politics and government—Juvenile literature. [1. Separation of powers. 2. United States—Politics and government.]
I. Title. II. Series.
JK305.K69 2004
320.473—dc21   2002009859

Manufactured in the United States of America
1 2 3 4 5 6 – DP – 09 08 07 06 05 04

independence from Great Britain. The colonists fought a bloody war and won their freedom.

The former colonies had become states. Together they formed a new national government. But that government could not get things done. It did not have enough power. Most Americans did not trust a strong government. They

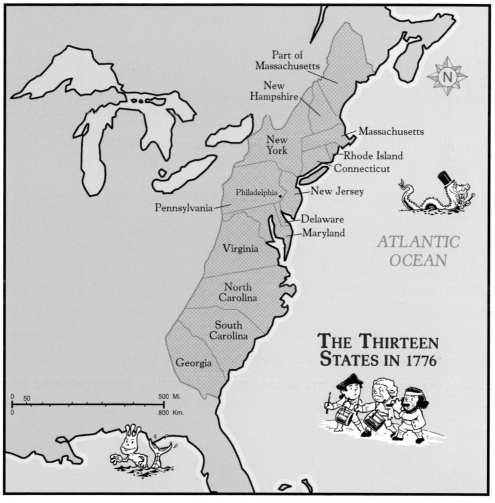

The total population of the thirteen new states in 1776 was about 1.5 million people.

worried that one person or group would gain too much power. What could they do?

The new country's leaders got together. They agreed on a new form of government. They wrote the details into a constitution, or set of laws.

The Constitution divides the federal, or central, government into three parts, or branches. The three branches are the legislative branch, the executive branch, and the judicial branch. Each part

Three Branches of Government

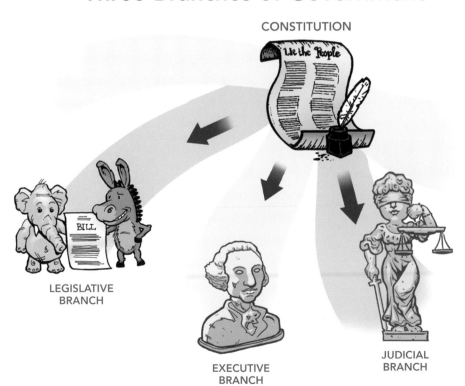

CONSTITUTION

LEGISLATIVE BRANCH

EXECUTIVE BRANCH

JUDICIAL BRANCH

DIG DEEPER If you worked for the federal government, which branch would you want to serve in?

of the government has different duties and powers. This is called separation of powers. Congress, the legislative branch, makes laws. The president, the executive branch, enforces laws. The courts, the judicial branch, interpret laws.

No branch does its job all alone. Each needs something from the others. And each branch can check, or limit, the power of the other branches. Together, they balance each other. This book is about this system, or plan, of checks and balances.

Why did the new nation's leaders choose this plan for running the federal government? Let's look back to 1787. We'll see why America's first government had trouble.

Do This!
Talk to your student council president to find out if your student council has a system of checks and balances. How does the council president share power with the other members of the council?

CHAPTER 1
PROBLEMS WITH THE
ARTICLES OF CONFEDERATION

(Above) Each state printed its own money in the early days of the American government.

TRUE OR FALSE? America's first national (central) government was a failure. The answer is True.

America's first government was based on the Articles of Confederation. The articles were written in 1777 and took effect in 1781. Each state had lots of power. The national government had very limited powers, and the congress of the

Confederation held most of it. Each of the thirteen states had one vote in the congress.

Under the Articles of Confederation, congress, not the people, chose the president. But the president had little power. Basically, he ran meetings for the congress.

Even the congress had little real power. The Articles did not require states to work together to solve national problems. Each state was more concerned with its own problems. The congress could not collect taxes. States agreed to give the congress

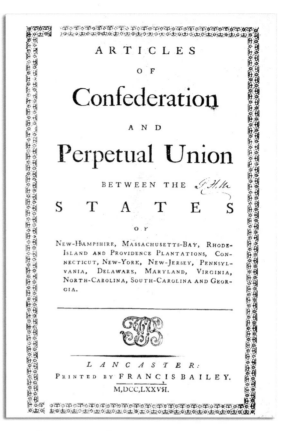

The Articles of Confederation were a set of laws that came before the U.S. Constitution.

some money, but they often paid late, or not at all. Without money, the government could not do much.

The congress could make treaties (agreements with foreign countries), but it could not force individual states to obey them. The congress could declare war and set up an army, but it could not make soldiers join.

The congress could not make laws for interstate commerce (business between people in different states). Each state acted like a separate country rather than as a part of one big country. As a result, America's businesses had problems.

To make matters worse, all thirteen states had to agree to any amendments, or changes, to the Articles of Confederation. That made change nearly impossible.

The former British colonies had become a new country, but its people were not unified. People thought of themselves as citizens of their own states first. They were Americans second.

THE CONSTITUTIONAL CONVENTION OF 1787

America's government needed fixing, so representatives from the states agreed to meet. Each state except Rhode Island sent delegates to Philadelphia, Pennsylvania. Rhode Island refused to send delegates because it did not want the national government to interfere with its affairs. The delegates met at Independence Hall. The Constitutional Convention went to work on May 25, 1787.

George Washington ran the meetings. For four months, delegates discussed problems with the Articles of Confederation. They explored solutions.

Seated in his "Rising Sun" chair *(above center)*, George Washington ran the meetings of the Constitutional Convention at Independence Hall *(right)*. For many delegates, the sun carved on the back of Washington's chair *(above his head)* symbolized their confidence that they could find a way to make the new nation's government work.

They borrowed ideas from different sources, such as Great Britain's government, their former colonial governments, and even ancient Greek philosophers, such as Aristotle and Plato.

The delegates worked long hours in the hot summer. They often argued with each other. By September, however, the delegates had agreed on a plan. They drafted (wrote) the Constitution. Unlike the Articles, the Constitution did not just set up a league (group) of states. The Constitution established a national government with authority over all citizens. The next step was getting states to accept the new Constitution.

PERSUADING THE PEOPLE

Many people worried about a strong national government. Without limits, it might take away citizens' rights and states' rights.

Three leading statesmen—James Madison, Alexander Hamilton, and John Jay—wanted to put people's minds

John Jay was one of the authors of *The Federalist: A Collection of Essays.* Unlike James Madison and Alexander Hamilton, Jay did not help write the Constitution.

at rest. They wrote letters to newspapers. The eighty-five collected letters were published as a book called *The Federalist* in 1787–1788. Topics included taxes, the army, state and federal relationships, and other issues. The letters favored a strong national government. That government would protect states' rights and people's rights too. Separation of powers was the key to protecting those rights.

The United States would have three branches of government under the new Constitution. These branches would be the legislative branch, the executive branch, and the judicial branch. No one branch would have all the power. But each branch would want to protect its own interests. That would make each branch police the others and keep them in line. The system

THE FEDERALIST: A COLLECTION OF ESSAYS, WRITTEN IN FAVOUR OF THE NEW CONSTITUTION, AS AGREED UPON BY THE FEDERAL CONVENTION, SEPTEMBER 17, 1787.

IN TWO VOLUMES.

VOL. I.

NEW-YORK:
PRINTED AND SOLD BY J. AND A. M'LEAN,
No. 41, HANOVER-SQUARE,
M,DCC,LXXXVIII.

The Federalist contains eighty-five letters in support of the Constitution.

would not be the most efficient one possible, but it would best prevent abuse of power.

Other issues came up, too. Critics wanted to be sure to protect people's personal rights. Those rights included freedom of speech, religion, and the press, rights in criminal cases, and other freedoms. They also wanted to protect the states' right to make their own laws, as long as they don't go against the Constitution. The Constitution's drafters added specific guarantees about individual and states' rights. These guarantees appear as the first ten amendments, or additions, to the Constitution. Together they form the Bill of Rights. After that was added, all the states agreed to the Constitution.

"SOUND BYTE" "The doctrine [idea] of the separation of powers was adopted by the convention of 1787, not to promote efficiency but to preclude [prevent] the exercise of arbitrary [unlimited] power." —Justice Louis D. Brandeis (1856–1941)

The Constitution gives us a strong national government. That government has thrived for more than two hundred years. America is very different than it once was, but separation of powers remains. Each branch checks and balances the power of the others. This system of checks and balances is very important. It works every day to protect Americans' freedom.

CHAPTER 2
CONGRESS AT WORK

QUICK QUESTION: Does Congress do anything besides make laws? The answer is yes. The Constitution gives Congress "all legislative Powers" of the national government. For example, Congress controls government taxes and spending. Congress regulates (controls) business with other countries and among the states. It has the power to issue money and set up the post office. Congress decides how many immigrants can become U.S.

(Above) Congress has the power to decide how much paper money to print.

New American citizens go to a naturalization ceremony that admits them to citizenship. Congress has the power to limit how many people from other countries may become American citizens.

citizens. Congress makes laws about authors' and inventors' rights. It decides what to do about crimes at sea or under international law. Congress sets up courts under the jurisdiction, or authority, of the Supreme Court. Only Congress—not the president—has the power to declare war and set up a national army. Congress also keeps the executive and judicial branches in check.

THE POWER OF THE PURSE

The Constitution gives Congress the "power of the purse." This means Congress controls government taxing and spending. This is a huge responsibility. The federal government's budget is about two trillion dollars a year.

That money pays for all federal agencies. Each agency is in charge of a certain field, such as banking or outer space. Most federal agencies are run by the executive branch. Each year they need money from Congress.

Suppose an agency, such as the National Aeronautics and Space Administration (NASA), acts against Congress's wishes. Congress can reduce NASA's funding (money) for future years, or it can get rid of one of its programs.

Astronaut Dale A. Gardner's sign is a joke. But he may have a good reason to worry about money. If Congress cuts too much money from NASA programs, the agency may want to hold a garage sale. Would you like to buy one of the satellites brought back on Gardner's space shuttle mission?

In this way, Congress could hold many government programs for "ransom" to get what it wants. But the president can veto, or reject, most budget bills. Instead, Congress and the executive branch often cooperate (work together) if they want a budget passed. The executive and legislative branches keep each other in check. This is an example of how the system of checks and balances works.

CONFIRMING PRESIDENTIAL APPOINTMENTS

The president chooses about seventy-five hundred people for various jobs. By law, the Senate must confirm (approve) several hundred of those appointments. These include ambassadors (U.S. representatives to

President Gerald Ford (*right*) appointed Shirley Temple Black (*lower left*) as the ambassador to Ghana in 1974. In 1989 President Ronald Reagan appointed Shirley Temple Black as the ambassador to Czechoslovakia. Both times, the Senate unanimously confirmed Black. She had been a popular movie star as a child in the 1930s (*upper left*).

foreign countries), cabinet members (department heads who advise the president), heads of federal agencies, and other high-ranking officials.

DIG DEEPER Who are your senators? Have they voted for or against nominations by the president? Most daily newspapers report votes in Congress.

The Senate examines the president's nominees (people chosen for a job). It checks their qualifications and character. It also looks at their views.

Sometimes the Senate confirms nominees quickly and easily. Other nominees get confirmation only after long hearings. The Senate rejects some nominees. Sometimes the president withdraws nominations due to criticism.

President Bill Clinton nominated Zoë Baird as attorney general (head of the Justice Department) in 1993. Baird had worked in the Justice Department and a law firm. She had become the head lawyer for a huge insurance company. But the Senate found out that Baird had not paid Social Security or filed certain legal papers for the nanny who took care of her children. Baird had broken the law, and critics questioned the nomination. Shouldn't the future attorney general obey the law? Faced with criticism, Clinton withdrew Baird's nomination. Janet Reno became attorney general instead.

Not every controversial (disputed) nomination gets blocked.

PEOPLE FILE The Senate unanimously confirmed Colin Powell as the first African American secretary of state in 2001. Powell's 35-year military career included service as a four-star general and chairman of the Joint Chiefs of Staff.

At a civil rights leadership conference in Washington, D.C., John Sweeney, a national labor leader, speaks out against John Ashcroft's nomination as attorney general.

Many senators questioned President George W. Bush's choice of John Ashcroft as attorney general. They wondered whether he would vigorously protect people's civil rights. Yet the Senate confirmed Ashcroft in 2001. In practice, the Senate approves most nominees, but the review process keeps the executive branch in check.

THE PRESIDENT'S STATE OF THE UNION ADDRESS TO CONGRESS

The U.S. Constitution calls for the president to report to Congress on "the State of the Union." The president's yearly State of the Union Address, delivered in January, sets goals for the year. The president can recommend legislation (laws) to Congress to achieve those goals. The president often proposes laws on other topics too.

TREATIES

The Constitution also says the president makes treaties, or agreements with foreign countries, for the United States. Treaties become effective only if the Senate ratifies (approves) them, however. For a treaty to be approved, a majority (more than 50 percent) of all senators must vote to ratify it. This is called a majority vote. Some treaties sail through the Senate. Others face heated debate. Still others get defeated.

In October 1963, President John F. Kennedy *(seated)* signed the Nuclear Test Ban Treaty between the United States, the Soviet Union, the United Kingdom, and France. These four countries were agreeing to stop test-firing nuclear weapons above ground, under water, and in outer space.

IMPEACHMENT

Impeachment is the act of charging a public official with serious wrongdoing. It is Congress's most drastic check against the president, judges, and other important government officials. Impeachment gives Congress a way to remove people from a public office (job).

The Constitution gives the House of Representatives (the House) the "sole Power of Impeachment." In other words, the House decides whether to bring charges against an official. A committee reviews the facts and writes the charges. Then the whole House votes on whether to impeach. Impeachment requires a majority vote.

Once someone is impeached, the Senate holds a trial. If the president is impeached, the chief justice of the United States runs the trial. After an impeachment trial, conviction removes someone from office. Conviction takes a two-thirds vote of the senators present. After that the government can prosecute (put someone on trial) for any crime. Congress can impeach federal judges, the president, the vice president, and members of the executive branch.

Did You KNOW? As of 2002, the Senate had convicted only seven federal judges of impeachment charges brought against them by the House.

When should individuals be impeached? The Constitution says "Treason, Bribery, or other high Crimes and Misdemeanors" are reasons to impeach. In other words, the wrongful act must be serious.

To date, the House has impeached only two presidents: Andrew Johnson in 1868 and Bill Clinton in 1998.

The Senate found both men innocent. President Richard Nixon resigned on August 9, 1974, just before his likely impeachment.

Impeachment is obviously a drastic limit on the abuse of power. Yet Congress's other checks and balances make a big difference too.

The House of Representatives impeached President Andrew Johnson *(top)*. To watch Johnson on trial in the Senate, people needed tickets *(bottom)*.

CHAPTER 3
THE PRESIDENT AND THE VETO POWER

TRUE OR FALSE? The president plays an important role in deciding which bills become law. The answer is True.

As head of the executive branch, the president's main job is enforcing the laws of the United States. But that's not the president's only job. The

(Above) In 1879 President Rutherford B. Hayes used his presidential power to veto an anti-Chinese bill. The bill would have limited the number of immigrants coming to the United States from China.

president limits Congress's actions with the veto power, or the power to say "no" to a law. Congress can override (overrule) a veto, but that is hard. The veto power gives the president an important say in which bills become law.

HOW THE VETO POWER WORKS

After both the House and Senate pass a bill by a majority vote, it goes to the president. The president gets ten days to sign or veto the bill. If the president signs the bill, it becomes a law. If the president does not like a bill, he or she vetoes it.

If the president vetoes the bill, it is returned to Congress. The president also sends along the reasons for vetoing the bill.

After a veto, Congress considers the bill again. Then it votes. If two-thirds of both the Senate and the House of Representatives vote for the bill, Congress overrides the veto. That means that the bill becomes law despite the veto.

DIG DEEPER The Constitution lets Congress override a veto by a two-thirds vote of the House and the Senate. Why is this an important check against the president's veto power?

What if the president doesn't sign or veto the bill? In most cases, the bill still becomes a law, just as if the president had signed it. But if Congress passes a bill less than ten days before it adjourns (quits working), then the president has fewer than ten days to make a decision. If the president does nothing in that time, then the bill is automatically vetoed. This do-nothing option is called the pocket veto. Presidents use this veto when they oppose a bill but don't want to veto it openly.

AVOIDING A DEADLOCK

With the veto power in place, how do laws get passed? What if the president belongs to one political party while most members of Congress belong to another political party? If the two parties have different goals, Congress may never create a bill that the president will sign. How can the federal government avoid a constant deadlock, or stalemate?

> ### THE LINE-ITEM VETO
>
> Suppose a president does not like part of a bill. Can he or she approve everything except that part? In 1996 Congress tried to give the president the power to do this. It was called a line-item veto. In 1998 the Supreme Court said the line-item veto was unconstitutional. Was the line-item veto a good idea?

The veto power gets Congress and the president to negotiate. Representatives of both branches of government meet often. Both groups know what bills are being considered. Both groups know each other's views.

If minor changes to a bill can avoid a veto, Congress may compromise. It may not get the exact bill it wanted. But it gets a law it can take credit for.

The president has reason to negotiate, too. No one wants to be known for always saying no. The president may also need Congress's support for other programs.

THE VETO IN ACTION

Presidents used the regular veto only thirty-four times before the Civil War. They used pocket vetoes only eighteen times during that same time.

Presidents used the veto power more often after the Civil War. As of 2003, presidents have used about 1,500 regular vetoes and 1,100 pocket vetoes.

So far, President Franklin Roosevelt holds the record for the most vetoes. From 1933 to 1945, Roosevelt made 372 outright vetoes and 263 pocket vetoes. In twelve years, Congress overrode only nine of his vetoes.

President Grover Cleveland held office from 1885 to 1889 and from 1893 to 1897. During those eight years, Cleveland made 346 outright vetoes and 238 pocket vetoes. Congress overrode only seven of Cleveland's vetoes.

That's why presidents often compromise on one bill to get support for another.

The veto power makes law-making more difficult than it might otherwise be. But that power lets the president keep Congress in check. In turn, Congress can override a veto by a two-thirds vote of both houses. That keeps the president from abusing his or her power.

President Grover Cleveland vetoed many bills.

CHAPTER 4
THE COURTS AND JUDICIAL REVIEW

QUICK QUESTION: Who has the last say on what the Constitution means? The answer is the federal courts.

The Constitution gives judicial power, or the power to judge, to the Supreme Court and other federal courts. In doing their job, courts conduct a judicial review. Judicial review lets courts interpret laws and decide if

This photograph of the Supreme Court in 1894 includes John Marshall Harlan *(above, seated second from right).* He served on the Supreme Court from 1877 to 1911. His grandson and namesake John Marshall Harlan was a Supreme Court justice too—from 1955 to 1971.

they are fair and if they follow the Constitution.

All branches of government have a duty to obey the Constitution. And the Supreme Court gets the last word on what the Constitution means.

JUDICIAL INDEPENDENCE

The Constitution's framers wanted judges to act fairly and use their best judgment, so they set up an independent judiciary. Federal judges are not elected. Therefore they do not need to worry if their decisions are unpopular with voters. Also, Congress cannot reduce federal judges' pay while they serve.

If a judge does something seriously wrong, Congress can impeach him or her. Unless he or she commits a crime, a federal judge can stay in office for life.

SHAPING THE LAW

Sometimes the law is clear. Then a court's job is simple. The trial judge decides what law applies in

AMENDING THE CONSTITUTION

The Supreme Court has the last word on what the Constitution means. But the Constitution can be amended, or changed, in two ways. Two-thirds of both houses of Congress (the Senate and the House of Representatives) can propose amendments. Or two-thirds of states can call a convention to do that. Either way, three-fourths of the states must agree to an amendment before it becomes part of the Constitution.

Amending the Constitution is not easy. Any amendment needs widespread support. Because no single state can block an amendment, however, the process is possible. Counting the Bill of Rights, the Constitution has had twenty-seven amendments so far.

During a trial, everyone has solemn responsibilities in a courtroom.

a case and tells the jury. The jury reviews the evidence and decides who wins. (If a case does not have a jury, the judge does both jobs.)

Sometimes laws are not clear. Often courts must interpret them, or decide what they mean. Court decisions shape the law's meaning. If any law conflicts with the Constitution, it cannot stand and will not be enforced.

JUDICIAL REVIEW IN ACTION

Judicial review checks Congress. The Supreme Court first established judicial review of laws in the case of *Marbury v. Madison* in 1803. At that time, the Court struck down part of an act of Congress. Since then the Court has thrown out many laws that go against the Constitution.

MARBURY V. MADISON

In the case of *Marbury v. Madison*, the Supreme Court held a federal law unconstitutional for the first time. Here is what happened.

President John Adams made dozens of court appointments just as his term ended. He appointed William Marbury as a judge for the District of Columbia. The Senate confirmed the appointment, making it official.

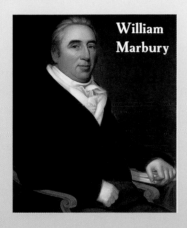

William Marbury

However, no one gave Marbury the final paper for his appointment before the incoming president, Thomas Jefferson, took office. Jefferson's secretary of state was James Madison. It was Madison's job to deliver the appointment paper, but he didn't. Madison and Jefferson wanted someone with their political views instead.

Without the paper, Marbury could not take the job. He asked the Supreme Court to make Madison deliver the paper. A law passed by Congress said that he could ask the Supreme Court to do that.

The Supreme Court said that Marbury had a lawful appointment, and Madison should have delivered the paper. However, the Court said the case did not belong in the Supreme Court. The law passed by Congress said Marbury could take it there. But the Court said the Constitution, not Congress, spelled out exactly which cases could start in the Supreme Court. Congress's law conflicted with the Constitution. Therefore, it did not count.

Neither Marbury nor Madison was happy. The Supreme Court criticized Madison for not delivering the paper. Marbury never got his job. But the Supreme Court was happy. It had the final word in deciding what the Constitution means. That is still our law.

Courts will not let either the president or federal agencies act against the Constitution. Judicial review also checks states' power. States cannot make or enforce laws that conflict with the Constitution. In this way, states cannot deprive citizens of their constitutional rights.

HOW DO THE JUSTICES DECIDE?

Just how do the federal courts decide what the Constitution means? There are two approaches to making the decision. One approach is called judicial restraint. It says judges should rule on constitutional issues only when they cannot avoid it. Judges with this view say that deciding political questions, or policy issues, is not their job. They say Congress or the president should decide such issues. For example, during the 1960s and early 1970s, the Vietnam War was controversial. But federal courts refused to say whether America's involvement in that war was constitutional.

American soldiers in combat in Vietnam

Judicial activism is the opposite view. Those who hold this view say judges can and should address policy questions. The case of *Brown v. Board of Education* is an example of judicial activism.

The case of *Brown v. Board of Education* involves the Fourteenth Amendment, which says all citizens deserve equal treatment under the law. But Kansas, the District of Columbia, and some other states had schools for African American children that were segregated, or separate, from other schools. Neither the executive nor the legislative branches would stop school segregation. It was up to the courts to do something. In 1954 the Supreme Court ruled that "separate, but equal" schools were unconstitutional. Racially segregated schools had to end.

The Supreme Court's order *(above)* in *Brown v. Board of Education* said public schools should admit all children without regard to race.

A President Tries to "Pack" the Supreme Court

When President Franklin Roosevelt became president in 1933, poverty was a major problem. Roosevelt asked Congress to pass laws to improve the economy. Those laws became known as Roosevelt's "New Deal."

Some programs created government jobs. Some programs built schools and parks. Some programs brought electricity to rural areas. Other New Deal laws dealt with farming and business.

Men work on a WPA (Works Progress Administration) project. The WPA was one of President Roosevelt's New Deal programs.

In 1935 the Supreme Court said some New Deal laws were unconstitutional. Roosevelt was outraged. How dare the Supreme Court's "old men" strike down his programs!

Roosevelt thought he had a way around the Constitution's checks and balances. In February 1937, Roosevelt asked Congress to let him appoint one new justice for each Supreme Court justice over age seventy. Six justices were already over seventy. The number of justices on the Court would have gone from nine to fifteen. Roosevelt would pick people who liked his programs, so a majority of the Supreme Court would be on his side.

© 1999 J.N. "Ding" Darling Foundation

In this political cartoon, President Franklin Delano Roosevelt (FDR) acts like a bossy ship captain. He orders his crew (Congress) to change the compass (the Supreme Court). (In reality, it is impossible to change the direction a compass points.)

Congress could have passed that law. Most likely, it would have been constitutional. Almost immediately, however, people objected. Roosevelt's plan to "pack" the Supreme Court with justices friendly to his views failed.

Judges soon retired from the Supreme Court. In the end, Roosevelt appointed six justices. Roosevelt got most of his New Deal programs, too. The United States kept its system of checks and balances.

CHECKS ON THE JUDICIARY

Both the president and Congress can check the power of the judicial branch. The president nominates, or picks, people to serve as federal judges. The Senate votes whether to confirm those nominations. The president usually picks members of his or her political party. Nominees usually agree with the president on many issues.

Usually, the Senate approves the president's choice. But the Senate does not automatically OK, or "rubber stamp," the nominations. The Senate Judiciary Committee holds hearings. The senators ask questions about the person's qualifications and opinions on different issues. Sometimes the nominee does not get confirmed. That happens about 20 percent of the time.

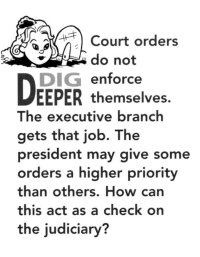

DIG DEEPER

Court orders do not enforce themselves. The executive branch gets that job. The president may give some orders a higher priority than others. How can this act as a check on the judiciary?

CONGRESS MAKES LAWS FOR THE COURTS

The Constitution gives Congress the power to set up federal courts under the jurisdiction of the Supreme Court. Congress decides how many courts to have and where those courts will be. Congress also decides what types of cases can go to those courts and how much money the courts get. These Congressional powers keep the courts from abusing their power.

Sometimes Congress can pass new laws in response to court decisions, too. If the courts say one law is too vague, Congress could write a more specific law.

THE POWER TO PARDON

Throughout history, kings and governors could pardon (forgive for committing a crime) convicted criminals. The Constitution also gives the president the power to pardon.

The executive pardon keeps courts from punishing people too harshly. Without it, Founding Father Alexander Hamilton said, courts' actions could be "too sanguinary [bloody] and cruel."

Congress and the president make many decisions that affect the courts. Together they have a say in who becomes a federal judge and how courts run. Together they balance the power of the judicial branch.

TURNING POINT In 1895 the Supreme Court ruled an income tax unconstitutional. In response, Congress proposed the Sixteenth Amendment. It was ratified in 1913 and says that Americans must file income tax returns by April 15 every year.

Did You KNOW? Since the adoption of the Constitution, presidents have granted about twenty-seven thousand pardons.

CHAPTER 5
THE STATES AND THE PEOPLE

TRUE OR FALSE? The three branches of national government have all the power in the United States. False! Under our system of government, states do many government jobs. Citizens play the most important role of all. In the end, all levels of American government must answer to the citizens.

(Above) Voters show support for New York Congressman Charles Schumer (center front). He is campaigning for a seat in the Senate.

STATE AND NATIONAL GOVERNMENT IN THE FEDERAL SYSTEM

The Constitution divides power between the national and state governments. This system is called federalism. Some powers are exclusive. They belong to just the states or just the national government. Other powers are shared. Both layers of government play a role.

What are some of the national government's exclusive powers? Only the national government can print money. Making treaties, declaring war, and regulating commerce (trade) between states are also exclusive powers of the national government.

The federal Department of Transportation is responsible for highway safety.

What are the powers that belong exclusively to the states? States establish local governments, like cities and counties. States issue licenses for driving and getting married. States set rules for practicing

In most states, a man and a woman wishing to marry must get a license from the state in which they live. Requirements vary from state to state.

States issue license plates for cars as well as licenses for drivers. In many states, clever car owners can choose to put a personal message on their plates by paying extra money.

Many people, including elected officials, run state and national governments. Here, Colorado voters hold signs for their favorite candidates for the U.S. Senate and for their state governor.

professions such as law or medicine. States run elections within their boundaries.

Both levels of government share some powers. The U.S. Environmental Protection Agency sets national standards for protecting the environment. States run programs to meet those standards within their states. Sometimes state standards may be even stricter.

Environmental Protection Agency employees wear special clothing to work at a hazardous materials site. Their agency cooperates with state officials.

Why divide power between national and state governments? Remember that the Founders did not trust a big central government. Federalism keeps each level of government from getting too much power.

The system also makes it easier to address local issues. As long as states follow the Constitution, they can adopt laws best suited to their needs. The Tenth Amendment protects states' rights. It says, "The powers not delegated to the United States by the Constitution, nor prohibited by it to the states, are reserved to the states respectively, or to the people." This amendment was adopted to reassure people that the national government would not take over the states.

HOW THE STATES ARE REPRESENTED

When the framers of the Constitution were discussing the legislative branch, states with fewer people wanted each state to have the same number of representatives. The larger states thought representation should be based on population, or the number of people living in the state. The two sides compromised. Each state—no matter its size—sends two people to the Senate. The number of people a state sends to the House of Representatives depends on the size of its population.

THE PEOPLE'S ROLE

Checks and balances under the Constitution are important, but the most important check on government comes from citizens. Citizens' greatest check on government rests in their right to vote. If the public loses confidence in the president, it can elect someone else. Likewise, people

This sign invites New York City's Spanish-speaking American citizens to "Vote here." It is an American citizen's responsibility to know where to go to vote.

can vote someone else into office if they are not happy with their representative, senator, or other elected official.

These officials all have limited, or set, terms of office. That means they serve for a specified number of years. If officials want to hold office for a longer time, they must be reelected by the people. Americans have many chances to change the makeup of their government. Public officials know they may not get reelected if they do not represent the voters well.

No single day of voting can completely change the federal government, however. At least two-thirds of the senators stay in power until the next federal election. And

"SOUND "A silent BYTE" majority [people who don't speak out or bother to vote] and government by the people are incompatible."
—Tom Hayden, twentieth-century political activist

In 2000 Hillary Rodham Clinton greets supporters in New York during her campaign for a seat in the U.S. Senate.

presidential elections come only every four years. This is important. It means that the federal government always has some continuity. The entire government can never be changed all at once. Even if there is a sudden, temporary swing in public opinion, the government stays stable.

Voters do not elect federal judges, but elections indirectly affect the courts. Presidents, who *are* elected by the voters, pick federal judges. If judges abuse their power, the public can call for Congress to act. Congress can make other laws to limit the power of the court. In severe cases, Congress can impeach a federal judge.

Voters have a strong voice in how government functions. The three separate branches of the federal government check and balance each other's power. The people have the final say.

WHAT CAN YOU DO?

Everyone can and should get involved with government. Your opinion counts. It counts even more when you have an *informed* opinion. Know what's going on with your government.

Keep up to date on political issues. Read the newspaper. Visit government and news sites on the Internet. Watch the news on television. Talk with parents, teachers, and other trusted adults. Ask questions.

When you have formed an opinion on an issue, tell people.

"SOUND BYTE" "If a nation expects to be ignorant and free, . . . it expects what never was and never will be."
—Thomas Jefferson

Write or e-mail the president. Contact your congressional representative and senator. Knowing your views affects how they vote.

Tell people outside of government, too. Write to the editor of your local newspaper. Perhaps you can persuade other people to agree with you. Then those people can also contact their elected representatives.

Exercise your right to vote as soon as you are old enough. Until then, encourage other citizens to vote.

Volunteers call people to remind them to vote.

Do This!

Write or e-mail the president or a member of Congress to share your opinion about something.

You might even volunteer to work for a favorite candidate. Who knows? One day you may even run for office!

The Constitution's first words are "We the people of the United States." Being an American citizen is a great privilege. It is also a big responsibility. The Preamble (introduction) to the U.S. Constitution refers to "the blessings of liberty." Do your part to ensure these blessings for all Americans.

YOUNG JOURNALIST SPEAKS UP

Twelve-year-old Ashley Williams of Alexandria, Virginia, wants to be a journalist when she grows up. She's starting her career early. On December 4, 2002, Ashley went to the White House to meet President George W. Bush. He was signing a bill that called for an Internet "Safe Zone" for kids twelve and under. After the signing, Ashley interviewed Senator Byron Dorgan of North Dakota. He had helped introduce the bill in Congress. Ashley stays informed. She's a reporter for *Time for Kids*, a news magazine for kids.

WHAT COULD THEY DO?

Have you ever played Rock, Paper, Scissors? Two players put out their hands at the same time. Hand gestures represent the three items. What gestures are shown determine the winner of each round. Scissors wins over paper, because scissors cuts paper. Rock wins over scissors, because rock smashes scissors. Paper wins over rock, because paper can cover the rock.

Checks and balances in American government are somewhat like this. Of course, the stakes are higher. Read each situation below. How could one or two other branches of government check an abuse of power?

> Congress passes a bill to let courts use evidence that was obtained illegally. But the Constitution forbids this. What can the president do? What can the federal courts do?

> The Supreme Court says a law making it a crime to loiter near federal buildings (hang around them too long without reason) is too vague. The Court says that makes the law unconstitutional. But Congress and the president disagree. What can Congress do? What can the president do?

> The president and attorney general want to stop terrorism. They have Justice Department officials bring people in for questioning. They hold the people for weeks without bringing charges. The people being held deny wrongdoing. Their families want them to come home. What can the federal courts do? What can Congress do?

CHECKS AND BALANCES
among the Three Branches of Government

LEGISLATIVE BRANCH

> Confirms judicial nominees
> Establishes federal courts under the authority of the Supreme Court
> Determines jurisdiction and pays for courts
> Has impeachment power
> Proposes constitutional amendments

> Exercises power of the purse
> Confirms appointments
> Ratifies treaties
> Can override vetoes
> Has impeachment power

JUDICIAL BRANCH

> Determines constitutionality of laws
> Interprets laws

EXECUTIVE BRANCH

> Proposes legislation
> Vetoes legislation
> Calls special sessions (meetings) of Congress when necessary

> Determines constitutionality of executive actions
> Interprets agency rules

> Appoints federal judges
> Grants pardons
> Enforces court orders

GLOSSARY

acquit: to find someone not guilty of a crime

Articles of Confederation: the document that organized America's first government after the Declaration of Independence

Constitution: the document that sets forth the organization of the government of the United States and lists protected rights for its citizens

executive branch: the part of the government relating to the president and agencies under him or her that enforce laws

federalism: division and sharing of powers by the state and national levels of government

impeachment: formal charges brought against the president, vice president, or other officials of the U.S. government by the House of Representatives

judicial branch: the part of government made up of the court system

judicial review: the courts' power to review the constitutionality of laws and of the actions of other branches of government at all levels

legislative branch: the part of the government that makes laws—the Senate and the House of Representatives at the federal level

nomination: the announcement of someone's name to fill a post (job)

presidential pardon: official forgiveness by the president for a crime

veto: presidential action rejecting a bill passed by Congress

SOURCE NOTES

For quoted material: p. 14, *Myers v. United States,* 272 U.S. 52, 293 (1926) (Brandeis, J., dissenting); p. 22, impeachment statistics cited in James MacGregor Burns, et al., *Government by the People,* 18th ed. (Upper Saddle River, NJ: Prentice-Hall, 2000), p. 35; p. 27, veto statistics from House of Representatives, Office of the Clerk, "Presidential Vetoes (1789–2001)," January 10, 2003 <http://clerk.house.gov/histHigh/Congressional_History/vetoes.php>, accessed April 9, 2003; p. 37, Hamilton quote from *The Federalist* (Cambridge, MA: Harvard University Press, 1966), Letter No. 74, p. 473; p. 37, statistics on presidential pardons from "Power of the Pardon Should Be Preserved," *San Francisco Chronicle,* March 4, 2001; p. 43, quoted in Sid Madwed, *Welcome to Sid Madwed's Collection of 26,388 Quotations for Speakers, Writers, and Communicators,* "Government," <http://www.madwed.com/Quotations/Quotations/Transfer__2/_Fear___Feasting___Feelings___/body___government___grace___gracefu.html>, accessed April 9, 2003.

BIBLIOGRAPHY

Bardes, Barbara A., Mack C. Shelley II, and Steffen W. Schmidt. *American Government and Politics Today: The Essentials.* 1994–1995 ed. St. Paul: West Publishing Company, 1994.

Biskupic, Joan, and Elder Witt. *The Supreme Court and the Powers of the American Government.* Washington, D.C.: Congressional Quarterly, 1997.

Burns, James MacGregor, et al. *Government by the People.* 18th ed. Upper Saddle River, NJ: Prentice Hall, 2000.

Casper, Gerhard. *Separating Power: Essays on the Founding Period.* Cambridge, MA: Harvard University Press, 1997.

Ducat, Craig R., and Harold W. Chase. *Constitutional Interpretation: Powers of Government.* 5th ed. St. Paul: West Publishing Company, 1992.

Fisher, Louis. *Constitutional Conflicts between Congress and the President.* Lawrence, KS: University Press of Kansas, 1997.

Foley, Michael, and John E. Owens. *Congress and the Presidency: Institutional Politics in a Separated System.* New York: Manchester University Press, 1996.

Gillers, Stephen. "Clinton's Chance to Play the King." *New York Times,* September 20, 1999.

Greenhouse, Linda. "Is Congress Forsaking Authority?" *New York Times,* May 14, 2000.

Jones, Charles O. *Separate But Equal Branches: Congress and the Presidency.* New York: Chatham House, 1999.

Kramer, Larry. "The Supreme Court v. Balance of Powers." *New York Times,* March 3, 2001.

Melusky, Joseph. *The American Political System: An Owner's Manual.* Boston: McGraw-Hill, 2000.

O'Brien, David M. *Constitutional Law and Politics: Struggles for Power and Governmental Accountability.* 4th ed. Vol. I. New York: W. W. Norton & Co., 2000.

Patterson, Thomas E. *We the People.* 2nd ed. New York: McGraw-Hill, 1998.

Power, Kerry, ed. *Democracy Owner's Manual.* Washington, DC: VOTE USA, Inc., 1995.

Rehnquist, William H. *The Supreme Court.* New York: Alfred A. Knopf, 2001.

Vile, M. J. C. *Constitutionalism and the Separation of Powers.* Indianapolis: Liberty Fund, 1998.

Wilson, Bradford P., and Peter W. Schramm. *Separation of Powers and Good Government.* Lanham, MD: Rowman & Littlefield, 1994.

FOR FURTHER READING

Benson, Michael. *Bill Clinton.* Minneapolis: Lerner Publications Company, 2004. Bill Clinton's two terms in office give readers a close-up look at the way the federal government is balanced.

Bonner, Mike. *How a Bill Is Passed.* Philadelphia, PA: Chelsea House Publishers, 2000. See how both the state and federal levels of government pass a law.

Feinberg, Barbara Silberdick. *The National Government.* New York: Franklin Watts, 1993. See how each branch of government works and learn why compromise plays an important role in our national government.

Feldman, Ruth Tenzer. *How Congress Works: A Look at the Legislative Branch.* Minneapolis: Lerner Publications Company, 2004. Learn how the Senate and House of Representatives work.

Kowalski, Kathiann M. *Order in the Courts: A Look at the Judicial Branch.* Minneapolis: Lerner Publications Company, 2004. This book examines how criminal and civil courts of law work.

Landau, Elaine. *The President's Work: A Look at the Executive Branch.* Minneapolis: Lerner Publications Company, 2004.
This book explores the president's many roles.

Maestro, Betsy, and Giulo Maestro. *The Voice of the People: American Democracy in Action.* New York: Lothrop, Lee & Shepard Books, 1996.
This books gives a good overview of how each branch of government does its job.

Roberts, Jeremy. *Franklin D. Roosevelt.* Minneapolis: Lerner Publications Company, 2003.
President Roosevelt's relationship with Congress during the Great Depression and World War II and his attempt to change the makeup of the Supreme Court provide great examples of our government's balance of power.

———*George Washington.* Minneapolis: Lerner Publications Company, 2004.
The author's lively explanation of Washington's role in the formation of our government sheds light on the workings of modern government.

Weber, Michael. *The Young Republic.* Austin, TX: Raintree Steck-Vaughn, 2000.
Understand the history behind our Constitution and its system of checks and balances.

Weizmann, Daniel. *Take a Stand! Everything You Ever Wanted to Know about Government.* Los Angeles: Price Stern Sloan, 1996.
Learn about our branches of government and how you can become an active and informed citizen.

WEBSITES

Ben's Guide to U.S. Government for Kids
<http://bensguide.gpo.gov>
This fun website features historical documents, information about government branches, games, and more.

C-Span
<http://www.cspan.org>
Learn the latest news about your national government on this fact-filled website.

Inside the Courtroom: Department of Justice (DOJ) USA Web Page for Kids
<http://www.usdoj.gov/usao/eousa/kidspage>
Learn about the law from lawyers themselves, with this site covering cases, legal terms, and more.

www.whitehousekids.gov
<http://www.whitehouse.gov/kids/>
Tour the White House with the president's dog, meet other executive branch pets, and read fun facts.

INDEX

ABOUT THE AUTHOR

Kathiann M. Kowalski has spent fifteen years practicing law. She holds a bachelor's degree in political science from Hofstra University. She received her law degree from Harvard Law School, where she was a member of the *Harvard Law Review*. Ms. Kowalski's books for young people include *Campaign Politics: What's Fair? What's Foul?* and *Hazardous Waste Sites*.

PHOTO ACKNOWLEDGMENTS

The photographs in this book are reproduced with the permission of: Virginia State Library and Archives, p. 4; © James Marrinan, p. 8; © Hulton|Archive by Getty Images, p. 9; Library of Congress, pp. 10–11 (LC-D416-28060), 12 (LC-D416-9856), 27 (LC-USZ62-7618); © A.A.M. Van der Heyden/Independent Pictures Service, p. 11; Beinecke Rare Book and Manuscript Library, Yale University, p. 13; © James Leynse/CORBIS SABA, p. 15; © Jim West, pp. 16, 46; NASA, p. 17; © Trinity Muller/Independent Picture Service, p. 18 (top); Courtesy of Gerald Ford Library, p. 18 (bottom); © AFP/CORBIS, p. 20; John F. Kennedy Library, p. 21; Minneapolis Public Library, p. 23 (top); © David J. & Janice L. Frent Collection/CORBIS, p. 23 (bottom); © CORBIS, p. 24; The Supreme Court of the United States, Office of the Curator, pp. 28, 31; © Photodisc, pp. 30, 39; U.S. Army Military History Institute, p. 32; National Archives, pp. 33 (NWCTB-267-PI139E21-10T1954 (JUDGEM)), 34 (NWDNS-RG-69-N-23478); © J.N. "Ding" Darling Foundation, p. 35; © Richard B. Levine, p. 38, 44; Minnesota State Historical Society, p. 40 (top); © Joseph Sohm/ChromoSohm Inc./CORBIS, p. 40 (bottom); © Michael D. Rieger/ZUMA Press, p. 41 (top); Courtesy of Environmental Protection Agency, p. 41 (bottom); © LeFranc/GAMMA/ZUMA Press, p. 43. The map on page 5 and the illustrations on pp. 6, 48, 49 are by Bill Hauser.